Editor Caroline Sheldrick
Designer John Cameron/Camron
Production Susan Mead

Acknowledgements

Graham Allen/Linden Artists Front cover, 10–11, 14–15, 20–21
David Astin/Linden Artists 8, 9, 18, 19, 22–23, 26, 27
Tim Hayward/Linden Artists 12–13, 30–31
Bob Hersey/Linden Artists 24–25, 38–39
Alan Male/Linden Artists 34–35
Robert Morton/Linden Artists 28–29, 32–33
John Rignall/Linden Artists 16–17, 36–37
Charlotte Snook 7, 40–41

Front cover: Badgers emerging from their sett at dusk.

Endpapers: Sunlight filters through the canopy of a mixed deciduous wood in summer.

Macdonald Educational Ltd
Holywell House
Worship Street
London EC2A 2EN

Printed in Hong Kong

ISBN 0 356 07122 7

NATURE IN FOCUS

THE WILDLIFE OF WOODLANDS

John Waters

Macdonald Educational

Contents

Introduction

There is much more to a wood than just trees. Woodlands provide a home or **habitat** for huge numbers of plants and animals which need each other to survive. The study of how they live together is called **ecology**.

We can think of woods as being divided into layers, rather like a house. The lowest layer, consisting of roots and soil, is the basement. Hordes of tiny creatures live in the soil. Mammals such as badgers and foxes dig burrows where they can shelter and give birth. Moles tunnel through the soil in search of food.

On the ground floor grow a great variety of wild flowers, as well as many grasses, ferns, mosses and toadstools. These ground-level plants provide food for small and large mammals, such as mice and deer. Most flowers depend on insects, such as bees, to pollinate them.

Above the ground layer, the first floor is occupied by shrubs and young trees, and is called the **shrub layer**. Here songbirds, such as warblers, search for insects hidden among the leaves and twigs. In the tangle of bushes birds are protected against attack by owls, hawks and other hunting birds.

The top floor is the **tree layer** where leafy branches form the woodland roof or **canopy**. Thousands of leaf-eating insects live in the trees. These in turn are eaten by birds, some of which nest high in the trees.

The tree trunks are like staircases which connect all the floors. Squirrels scamper up them to escape from enemies on the ground and to explore the tree tops for food. Cracks and crevices in the bark shelter hundreds of insects. Trunk holes are nest sites for many bird species.

A spreading network of roots anchors the tree firmly to the ground and pumps soil water and minerals up through the trunk and into the branches, twigs and leaves. As with all green plants, the leaves use sunlight to make sugars which provide energy. These sugars combine with water and minerals which enable the trees to grow.

Woodlands are **ecosystems** which bustle with life. They are places of great natural beauty but are also very important in other ways. They provide us with timber, shelter crops from the wind, and protect the soil from being washed away by the rain.

▼ **Visiting a wood. Wild animals and birds are easily scared away, so if you want to see them, wait in a dry, sheltered place for about half an hour. You will see far more if you keep still and quiet.**

Leaf or needle?

Different kinds of tree

Two main types of forest grow in Europe. **Broad-leaved** forests grow in western and central Europe, while **coniferous** forests are usually found further north. Most broad-leaved trees are **deciduous** which means they lose their leaves in autumn and grow new ones the next spring. Coniferous forests are made up of **evergreen** trees which keep their leaves all the year round. They shed old needles and grow new ones continuously.

Water flows constantly up the tree from the roots and is lost through the leaves. In winter the roots cannot draw enough water from the cold soil. Broad-leaved trees drop their leaves to save water. Coniferous trees have waterproof leaves, and can therefore live further north and in mountains.

The shape of trees

Broad-leaved trees have a few large branches or limbs which sprout from the trunk and grow upwards to form the crown. Conifers have tall and slim trunks with many side branches. Their thin, flexible branches can bend under the weight of snow then spring up again without snapping.

Conifers grow very close to each other; a coniferous forest is quite dark inside.

Timber

Broad-leaved trees are also called **hardwoods** because their timber is very strong. Most hardwoods, such as oak or beech, grow very slowly and are not cut for timber until they are about a hundred years old. Conifers are called **softwoods**; they grow much faster and can be cut after only fifty years.

▲ The leaves of broad-leaved trees are arranged so that they catch as much sunlight as possible. The green pigment uses light and water to make food for the tree.

▲ Like most broad-leaved trees, conifers depend on the wind to carry male pollen to the female parts. When the female cone is ripe it splits and the seeds fall out.

▲ If the trunk of a conifer such as a pine is damaged, sticky resin oozes from the wound. This gums up insect pests that might otherwise bore holes in the wood.

Our varied woodlands

Woods and plantations

Long ago Europe was covered by dense forest. There are now very few ancient forests left. Most of the woodlands of today are greatly changed from their natural state; many have been planted. In **plantations**, the trees are the same age because they were planted at the same time.

Natural woodlands contain a mixture of tree species (kinds of tree), but usually one is more common than the rest. This is the **dominant species**. It grows better than the rest because it thrives on the type of soil found there. Oak trees do well on heavy, fertile, clay soils. Beech grows best on light, chalky soils and ash is often dominant on limestone hillsides. Conifers are found growing on thin, poor soils. Dense birch woods grow well on heaths and waste ground.

The canopy

Oak and ashwoods usually form an open canopy. The gaps between the trees and their leaves let light through, so many plants can grow in the shrub and ground layers. Beech forms a very dense canopy; this makes the ground below very shady with few plants growing. In conifer plantations it may be so dark that the only ground plants are fungi which do not need light to grow.

Using woodlands

Foresters cut woodlands in a number of ways. A tree may be **coppiced** by cutting it at ground level. It does not die and in time several new shoots grow from the stump. These can be cut later for poles. Deer were fenced out of coppiced woodland because they ate the bark and young shoots. In Royal hunting forests where deer roamed free the trees were cut 2–3 metres above the ground out of their reach. This is called **pollarding**.

▲ Some of the finest beechwoods grow on the steep slopes of chalk hills where they are called beech hangers.

▲ Modern conifer plantations have machines to cut down the trees, carry the timber and dig trenches for the new crop of trees.

▲ Hazel coppice was cut about every 7 years to provide poles which were split and woven into hurdle fences for sheep pens.

▲ Pollarded trees, such as these hornbeams, grow a cluster of branches where the trunk was cut. Pollarded willows are most familiar.

Looking up in broad-leaved woodland

Trees forming the woodland canopy and the bushy undergrowth of shrubs and saplings are rich in wildlife. An ability to climb or fly helps animals to explore habitats above the ground.

The grey squirrel (15) is an athletic climber. Long, sharp claws on its toes enable it to keep a grip, even on the smooth bark of beech trees. When alarmed it races up into the tree tops, jumping between branches with great skill.

Many woodland birds nest in tree holes. This protects them from predators such as jays (19) which are ruthless nest-robbers. Jays watch parent birds closely to find where they are nesting then steal the eggs and chicks.

Some birds search for food on tree trunks. Cracks and crevices in the bark harbour thousands of insects.

▲ The **female leaf-rolling weevil** (30) cuts and rolls hazel leaves into an egg container.

Key		11	Hawthorn	23	Tree creeper
		12	Ivy	24	Tawny owl
1	Oak	13	Honeysuckle	25	Redstart
2	Beech	14	Bracket fungus	26	Wren
3	Hornbeam	15	Grey squirrel	27	Bees
4	Ash	16	Wild boar	28	Purple emperor
5	Small-leaved elm	17	Fallow deer		butterfly
6	Sycamore	18	Wood pigeon	29	Purple hairstreak
7	Wild cherry	19	Jay		butterfly
8	Sweet chestnut	20	Pied flycatcher	30	Leaf-rolling weevil
9	Hazel	21	Nuthatch	31	Lichen moth
10	Maple	22	Green woodpecker	32	Hawfinch

leg hairs

▲ **Wild bees (27)** collect pollen from flowers and feed it to the larvae in the hive. The bee rolls the pollen into lumps which stick to hairs on the hind legs.

▼ The fore-wings of **lichen moths (31)** have the same colour and pattern as lichen. During the day they rest on lichen-covered tree trunks, safe from predators.

The nuthatch (21) is unusual; it crawls head first down the tree, where other birds climb upwards. Beside insects it also eats beech nuts and acorns; it wedges them into a crack before hammering them open with its bill.

The pied flycatcher (20) flies from its perch in the trees, chasing flying insects. The redstart (25), like the pied flycatcher, is a migrant from Africa and also lives chiefly on insects snapped up on the wing. The males display their bright red tail feathers to attract females.

Brightly coloured wings of butterflies also serve to attract mates. The purple emperor (28) and purple hairstreak (29) both live high in the tree tops.

◄ The **hawfinch (32)** has a massive beak with which it can crack open cherry stones, one of its favourite foods, in autumn and winter.

Trees of broad-leaved woodland

Broad-leaved woodland trees can be identified by their form, the shape of their leaves, and appearance of the bark. Some produce small green flowers which are wind pollinated and others have colourful blossom to attract insects. The great variety of seeds, nuts and berries provides food for many woodland animals.

*Not to scale

▲ **Hornbeam** Deciduous
A hornbeam has very hard wood. The leaves and bark may be mistaken for beech but the seeds are each joined to a thin leafy sail which carries them on the wind. The male and female catkins appear in March.

▲ **Sweet Chestnut** Deciduous
The flowers appear in July, later than on most trees, and are pollinated by insects. The glossy brown nuts fall from their spiny cases during October. They are very good to eat. Chestnut is often coppiced for fence posts.

▲ **Beech** Deciduous
The beech has smooth grey bark and grows over 40 metres high. The nuts are called beech-mast, are shed in October, and provide food for many animals. The leaves are very pale in spring, and turn bright gold in autumn.

▲ **Oak** Deciduous
The mighty oak can live for over a thousand years. It has deep roots and thick rough bark. The green flowers open in April or May and the acorns fall in autumn. Many birds and mammals eat acorns.

From acorn to oak tree

The mature oak tree may weigh more than 30 tonnes yet it starts life as an acorn weighing a few grams. Germination takes place in the spring. The acorn case cracks open and roots push down into the soil. The shoot grows up towards the light and soon the first pair of leaves unfurl.

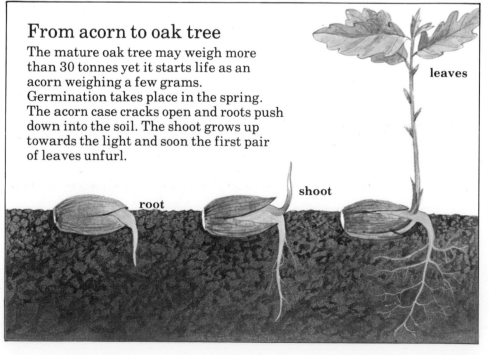

leaves

shoot

root

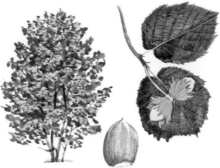

▲ Hazel Deciduous
Hazel is a very common species in the shrub layer. It has smooth brown bark. The flowers are wind-pollinated. They appear in February, long before the leaves. Hazel nuts are eaten by many animals.

▲ Holly Evergreen
Holly has shiny, prickly leaves. The trunk is covered with smooth, grey bark but the twigs are green. It flowers in May. The bright red berries ripen in September but stay on the tree throughout winter.

▲ Sycamore Deciduous
Sycamore grows very fast and is abundant in many woods. Yellowish flowers appear in April. They are rich in nectar and very attractive to bees. Squirrels are fond of nibbling the bark because the sap is sweet.

▲ Field maple Deciduous
A small tree, growing to about 10 metres. The leaves are the same shape as sycamore's but smaller. Many insects suck the sweet sap from the leaves. The flowers open in May with the leaves.

▲ Wild cherry Deciduous
Cherry has smooth, purple-brown bark. The large, white flowers blossom in April or May and are pollinated by bees. The cherries ripen during the summer and they are greedily eaten by birds.

▲ Hawthorn Deciduous
Hawthorn has sharp thorns on the twigs and branches. The white flowers, called May blossom, are sweet-scented to attract insects which pollinate them. The red berries are a favourite food of birds.

▲ Ash Deciduous
Ash has pale grey bark. In April the flowers appear in large green clusters before the leaves open. After pollination by wind, bunches of ash seeds or 'keys' are formed. Ash grows best in moist, fertile soils.

On the ground in broad-leaved woodland

Colourful wild flowers carpet the woodland floor wherever enough sunlight shines through the trees' leafy canopy. Many animals live or hide under fallen branches. The wood becomes riddled with holes made by the numerous insect larvae feeding on the dead wood. Old tree stumps are good places to look for fungi and mosses.

Butterflies fly in the summer. The speckled wood (**29**) and ringlet butterflies (**31**) settle on grasses after mating and lay their eggs. The white admiral (**30**) visits bramble flowers to feed on nectar.

The pygmy shrew (**19**) is Europe's smallest mammal. Nearby is a common shrew (**18**); they both hunt on the ground in a ceaseless search for food. They eat tiny animals living amongst leaf litter or in the soil, such as millipedes (**32**), centipedes (**34**), earthworms (**35**) and woodlice (**33**). Earthworms are very plentiful in woodland soil and the mole (**17**) digs underground tunnels to catch them.

The truffle (**38**) is a curious fungus that grows underground. It has a strong aroma which attracts mammals such as badgers, squirrels, hedgehogs and mice. They dig up and eat the fungus and spread its spores in their droppings.

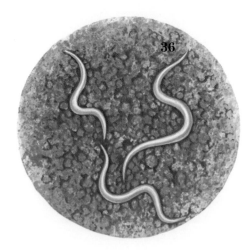

◀ **Nematodes** are tiny thread-like worms a few millimetres long. A teaspoonful of soil contains hundreds of them. They feed on dead plant and animal remains in the soil.

▶ **Worms** surface at night to take in leaves and other food, and to mate. Holding tight to its hole with the bristles on its body, the front end sweeps from side to side until it finds something good to eat. The worm cast is digested soil.

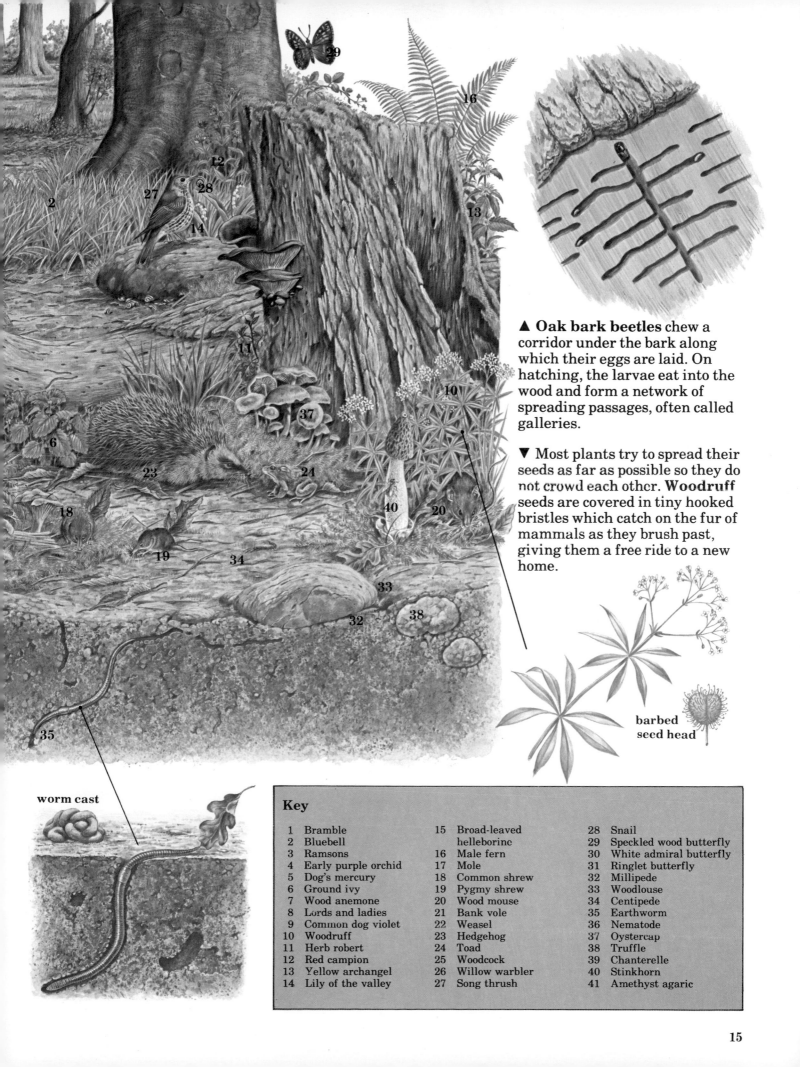

▲ **Oak bark beetles** chew a corridor under the bark along which their eggs are laid. On hatching, the larvae eat into the wood and form a network of spreading passages, often called galleries.

▼ Most plants try to spread their seeds as far as possible so they do not crowd each other. **Woodruff** seeds are covered in tiny hooked bristles which catch on the fur of mammals as they brush past, giving them a free ride to a new home.

barbed seed head

worm cast

Key

1	Bramble	15	Broad-leaved helleborine	28	Snail
2	Bluebell	16	Male fern	29	Speckled wood butterfly
3	Ramsons	17	Mole	30	White admiral butterfly
4	Early purple orchid	18	Common shrew	31	Ringlet butterfly
5	Dog's mercury	19	Pygmy shrew	32	Millipede
6	Ground ivy	20	Wood mouse	33	Woodlouse
7	Wood anemone	21	Bank vole	34	Centipede
8	Lords and ladies	22	Weasel	35	Earthworm
9	Common dog violet	23	Hedgehog	36	Nematode
10	Woodruff	24	Toad	37	Oystercap
11	Herb robert	25	Woodcock	38	Truffle
12	Red campion	26	Willow warbler	39	Chanterelle
13	Yellow archangel	27	Song thrush	40	Stinkhorn
14	Lily of the valley			41	Amethyst agaric

Wild flowers

Wild flowers are the most colourful feature of the woodland ground layer. Bright petals and scents attract insects which pollinate the flowers. In some woods a few species, such as dog's mercury, bluebell and bramble are dominant.

*Not to scale.

▲ **Bluebell** Flowers April–June
Bluebells grow from a white, juicy bulb and they are very common in woods. The hanging clusters of bell-shaped flowers are sometimes pink or white. The stem grows about 30 cm tall, and when broken oozes a sticky juice.

▲ **Primrose** Flowers Feb–May
The primrose is a common early spring flower in woods and shady places. It has a rosette of soft, wrinkled leaves. The pale yellow flowers are borne on slender, pinkish stalks, growing about 10 cm tall.

▲ **Ramsons** or **Wood garlic**
Flowers April–June
Ramsons grows from a bulb and forms large patches in moist woods. Related to the onion family, the leaves smell strongly of garlic. The white flowers grow in clusters.

▲ **Bramble** Flowers June–September
Brambles have very long, spreading stems. Sharp thorns on the stems and hooked prickles under the leaves protect them from deer. Many mammals and birds eat the blackberries in autumn.

▲ **Wood anemone** Flowers March–April
The wood anemone flowers before tree foliage shades the woodland floor. The delicate white flowers are tinged with pink. The stems are slightly hairy and grow about 20 cm high.

▲ **Common violet** Flowers April–June
Violets have heart-shaped leaves and rarely grow taller than 10 cm. The lower petals are marked with fine dark lines which guide insects to the nectar in the centre of the flower. The flowers have a pleasant, sweet smell.

The art of pollination

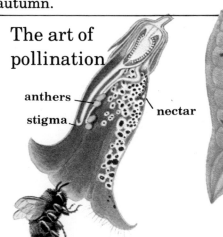

anthers

stigma

nectar

Foxgloves attract bumble bees with their colour and scent of nectar. As a bee crawls up the flower tube, pollen sticks to it, pollinating the next foxglove.

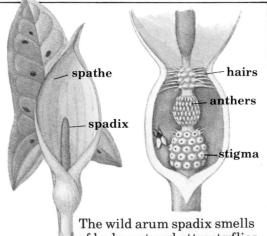

spathe

hairs

spadix

anthers

stigma

The wild arum spadix smells of bad meat and attracts flies. They slip down the spathe and are trapped. Their movements transfer pollen to the stigmas. Next day the hairs shrivel and they can fly away.

Broad-leaved helleborine
Flowers July–September
This plant grows to about one metre high. It does well in beech woods but also appears in conifer plantations. The flowers are pollinated mainly by wasps. ▼

Broad-leaved helleborine

Early purple orchid

▲ Wood sorrel Flowers April–May
Wood sorrel is a small, delicate plant that grows in shady woods. The leaves fold tightly shut at night and they have a sour taste like rhubarb. The pale white petals are marked with pink streaks.

Dog's mercury Flowers March–April
Dog's mercury is particularly common in woods growing on rich soil. The greenish-yellow flowers are borne on stalks about 3 cm long. The leaves are poisonous. ▼

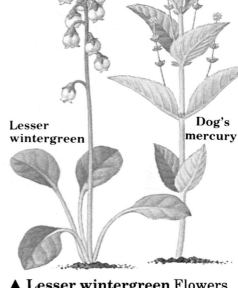

Lesser wintergreen

Dog's mercury

▲ Early purple orchid Flowers April–May
Early purple orchids are especially common in coppiced woodland. The leaves are marked with dark blotches and the flowers vary in colour from faint pink to deep purple.

▲ Bilberry Flowers April–June
Bilberry can form thick carpets on the floor of coniferous woods, especially if the soil is sandy. It has woody stems and small leaves. The berries are edible.

▲ Lesser wintergreen Flowers June–August
Lesser wintergreen is found in shady pine forests. Clusters of round, pink flowers hang from a stalk growing to about 20 cm tall.

▲ Herb paris Flowers May–July
Herb paris is an unusual plant which grows on fertile, chalky soils. Each plant has just four broad leaves and produces only one green flower. The fruit is a black berry. Herb paris belongs to the Lily family.

▲ Herb robert Flowers April–October
Herb robert is a common woodland plant and flowers throughout the summer. The stems are usually red and slightly hairy. It often grows in dense clumps to a height of 30 cm.

▲ Ground ivy Flowers March–June
Ground ivy is a low, creeping plant whose flowers are among the first to appear in spring. It has a square stem from which sprout pairs of dark green, wrinkled leaves that have a strong, bitter smell.

Spring

In spring the forest wakes up from its long winter sleep. The new leaves of plants grow quickly before the trees come into leaf and shade them. Birds' songs fill the forest. Each attracts a mate and warns other birds off a territory. At night owls hoot through the trees. Tawny owls now lay their white eggs in a hollow tree. Woodpeckers drill their nest-holes; song thrushes collect mud to line their nests. Great tits often use a woodpecker's hole and lay their eggs on a soft bed of feathers. Birds bring food to their mates as they sit on the eggs.

Squirrels search the ground for any nuts left over from winter. When alarmed they sprint up into the tree tops and leap from branch to branch. Dormice leave their snug nests under tree roots. They have eaten their winter store of nuts and must now search for buds and shoots. At night, newly-woken hedgehogs shuffle through the leaves looking for snails and beetles.

Animals are born in spring so they can feed on the plentiful summer food. Roe deer give birth to two fawns and leave them hidden among bushes while they feed. In deep, underground burrows badger cubs and fox cubs suckle their mother's milk. Toads crawl to the nearest pond to breed. The females lay long necklaces of spawn.

Beetles crawl out of cracks in tree trunks; larvae and caterpillars hatch from tiny eggs and start feeding. Bird migrants peck at them hungrily.

By the end of spring the ground is carpeted with wild flowers. The green flowers of trees shower vast amounts of pollen into the wind. The longer days signal the trees to burst into leaf; the cool and shady woodland summer has arrived.

▲ Celandines and primroses are among the first flowers to appear in the spring.

▲ The dormouse is a good climber. Its long bushy tail helps it to balance on thin twigs as it nibbles buds.

▲ Young roe deer are called fawns. Their coats are dappled with light brown blotches so they match their background.

▲ The squirrel's drey is a huge ball of leaves and twigs. Here they give birth to 3 or 4 young in April.

Summer

In summer the woods are buzzing with life. Bees are busy visiting flowers to collect nectar and pollen to feed their larvae. The trees and bushes are in full leaf; their juices provide food for many insects. Some larvae burrow inside the leaf; they are called leaf-miners. Caterpillars spend all day chewing leaves. Leaf-cutting bees neatly bite off pieces of leaf to build their nests. Wasps chew tiny bits of wood to a pulp with which they make their paper-thin homes.

Butterfly and moth pupae cases crack open; the adults crawl out, stretch and dry their wings, then fly away. Butterflies flutter in sunny clearings to attract a mate. Their tiny eggs are laid on those plants which the caterpillars will eat. At night moths are chased by bats around the tree tops. In the early morning spiders mend any holes in their webs; wind and rain can wreck them so they often have to build new ones.

Gnats and midges above the tree tops may be snapped up by pied flycatchers. Birds are busy collecting food for their young. The chicks are always hungry. Cuckoos lay their eggs in the nests of other birds, especially warblers. The weary parents spend all day feeding the greedy young cuckoo which soon grows much bigger than themselves. Many seed-eating birds also feed their young on insects; they are so plentiful and the chicks' beaks are too soft for seeds.

Slugs and snails leave slimy trails over the ground and on the leaves they eat. Tree slugs crawl up trees to eat lichens on the bark.

Fox cubs play at the entrance to the earth in late evening. At dusk the vixen trots off to catch rabbits, mice and birds. She shares her meal with the cubs who will soon be hunting for themselves.

▲ A pair of willow warblers catch hundreds of caterpillars each week to feed their hungry young.

▲ Baby hedgehogs have very soft spines so they do not prickle their mother while suckling her milk.

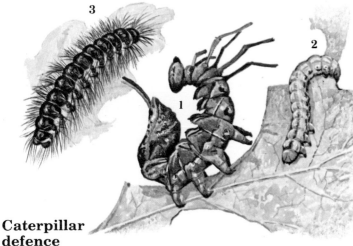

Caterpillar defence
1. Lobster moth rears up and squirts acid at its attackers; 2. Winter moth is camouflaged; 3. Oak processional has poison-tipped bristles.

▲ The female gall wasp lays her eggs on an oak twig bud. An oak marble grows around it and the larva feeds on the spongy tissue.

Mammals

Mammals are warm-blooded vertebrates. Their fur coats keep them warm, especially in winter. After mating, the babies develop inside their mother until they are born. They suckle her milk until they are old enough to feed themselves.

*Not to scale. Average adult body length given.

▲ **Wild boar** 150cm tail 25cm
Wild boars are armed with dangerous tusks. They rummage through the woods for acorns, roots and bulbs. The sow gives birth to up to 12 young in April or May. Boars are increasingly common in parts of Europe.

▲ **Badger** 75cm tail 18cm
Badgers leave their setts at dusk. They are very clean animals and dig their toilet pits away from the sett. Eating almost anything, they use their long claws to dig for worms, roots and bulbs. Up to 4 cubs are born in March.

▲ **Grey squirrel** 26cm tail 21cm
The grey squirrel was introduced from America last century and is now very common. It eats buds, bark, leaves and shoots and stores nuts in winter. Up to 4 young are born in spring in a leafy nest or drey. It does not have ear tufts.

▲ **Red squirrel** 25cm tail 21cm
The red squirrel is a native European animal. It is found in pine woods and the seeds of fir-cones are one of its favourite foods. It will also eat nuts, berries, mushrooms and birds' eggs. It is no longer as common as the grey squirrel.

▲ **Pine marten** 45cm tail 25cm
The pine marten has a slim body, sharp claws and a long bushy tail which help it clamber easily through the tree branches. It hunts squirrels, birds and small mammals. Large numbers have been trapped for their fur and they are now quite rare.

▲ **Wood mouse** 9cm tail 9cm
Wood mice breed several times in summer. The young mice grow quickly and leave the nest when they are only 2 weeks old. They eat plants and store nuts and seeds for winter. They are common throughout Europe.

▲ **Bank vole** 10cm tail 4.5cm
The bank vole builds a nest of grass and moss on the ground or under a log. There are up to 6 young in each litter. They feed mostly on grass seeds and berries but will also eat snails and insects.

▲ **Common shrew** 7cm tail 5cm
The common shrew is active by day and night all the year round. It has a long whiskered snout for sniffing out worms and insects. It feeds mostly under ground. The common shrew has a very shrill squeak.

▲ **Red deer** 200cm tail 15cm
Red deer live in herds and feed on grasses, mosses, shoots and buds. The stags shed their antlers in winter and grow a new set during spring. Red deer mate in September but the young are not born until spring.

▲ **Roe deer** 130cm tail 4cm
Roe deer are common in Europe. They live in small family groups and feed on grasses, shoots and leaves. They run with great bounding strides when alarmed, and are good swimmers. They feed at dawn and dusk.

▲ **Fallow deer** 135cm tail 18cm
Many centuries ago fallow deer were introduced into royal hunting forests to provide sport. They eat leaves, bark, nuts and berries. Two fawns are born in May or June. In winter the white spots on its coat disappear.

▲ **Weasel** 30cm tail 8cm
The weasel is bloodthirsty and fearless. It will attack animals much larger than itself, such as rabbits. Mice, voles and young birds are also eaten. Up to 6 young are born in spring and the mother defends them bravely.

▲ **Hedgehog** 28cm tail 3cm
The hedgehog rolls into a ball when frightened but it can run quite quickly despite having short legs. It eats worms, insects and small mammals. It sleeps during the day and hibernates in winter.

▲ **Fox** 80cm tail 40cm
The fox is a cunning hunter, creeping quietly towards its prey before pouncing. It eats mostly small mammals and birds and sometimes insects, especially beetles. It often lives in the same burrow as a badger.

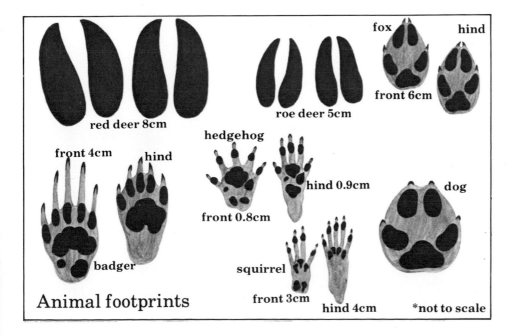

red deer 8cm

roe deer 5cm

fox   hind

front 6cm

front 4cm   hind

hedgehog

hind 0.9cm

front 0.8cm

badger

dog

squirrel

front 3cm   hind 4cm   *not to scale

Animal footprints

▲ **Mole** 15cm tail 3cm
The mole has short, dark, velvety fur. With its large forepaws it digs tunnels in search of worms and insects. It is almost blind and finds food by smell. Molehills show where a mole has pushed soil from its tunnel.

21

Day and night

The sun provides light and warmth for animals which feed and hunt during the day. These are called *diurnal* animals. *Nocturnal* animals are suited for a life in the dark and they become active at night.

Most birds wake at dawn and search for food throughout the day. Pheasants (**14**) peck on the ground eating seeds and shoots. A blue tit (**13**) looks for insects hidden under the leaves. The sparrowhawk (**10**) seizes a chaffinch in mid-air.

Most flying insects become active as the sun climbs in the sky. Butterflies flutter around the wood's edge visiting flowers to sip the sweet nectar. A spider waits for flies to blunder into its silky web.

An adder (**9**) basks in the sunshine before going hunting.

hornet

hornet clearwing moth

◀ Unlike most moths the **hornet clearwing moth** is active during the day. It avoids being eaten by birds because it looks just like a hornet wasp which stings.

▶ The **brimstone butterfly** is one of the few that hibernate. It spends the winter months hidden among dead leaves and emerges during the first sunny days of spring.

The nightingale (**28**) sings from a hawthorn bush at night when other forest songbirds are asleep. Hundreds of nightflying moths are also seeking a mate.

▲ The **long-eared bat**, like all bats, has poor eyesight but it can find food in the dark because it emits sound waves which bounce off flying moths. Its huge ears listen for the echoes so it can close in for the kill.

▼ The **great green bush cricket** lurks among plant stems and pounces on insects. At dusk the males rub their wings together to make a chirping sound which attracts females. Their ears are not on their heads but on their legs! When frightened they jump into the air and glide to the ground on fluttering wings.

Bank voles (**8**) scurry through the undergrowth looking for wild strawberry (**7**) fruits. Rabbits (**5**) feed in the grassy clearing unaware that they have been spotted by a weasel (**6**).

As night falls roe deer leave the shelter of trees to feed. Many of the larger mammals are nocturnal. Badger cubs play around the sett entrance.

Key					
			12	Long-eared owl	22 Fox
			13	Blue tit	23 Roe deer
1	Oak	4 Bracken	14	Pheasant	24 Hornet
2	Bramble	5 Rabbit	15	Brimstone butterfly	25 Hornet clearwing moth
3	Hawthorn	6 Weasel	16	Wood white butterfly	26 Tawny owl
7	Wild strawberry		17	Silver-washed fritillary	27 Nightjar
8	Bank vole		18	Garden spider	28 Nightingale
9	Adder		19	Long-eared bat	29 Spurge hawk moth
10	Sparrowhawk		20	Pipistrelle bat	30 Goat moth
11	Chaffinch		21	Badger	31 Great green bush cricket

Birds

Birds are warm-blooded and covered with feathers which make up their *plumage.* In many species the male or cock bird has a more colourful plumage than the female or hen. The young are fed by their parents until ready to leave the nest. The great variety of bird calls and songs are a striking feature of woodland.

*Not to scale. Average adult body length given.

▲ **Chaffinch** 15 cm
The chaffinch is very common in Britain. A cup-shaped nest is built in a fork of a tree or bush in April or May. They feed the young with insects in summer but eat mainly seeds at other times.

▲Great tit 14 cm
The great tit is easily recognized by the black band which runs from its chin to its tail. It nests in tree holes and will use nest boxes. It eats insects, nuts and seeds. The song sounds like 'tea-cher tea-cher'.

▲ **Jay** 34 cm
The jay is a shy but handsome bird with its pinkish plumage and bright blue wing patches. It eats eggs, young birds, insects, snails and seeds. In autumn it stores hundreds of acorns for the winter.

▲ **Sparrowhawk** Male 28 cm
Female 38 cm
The sparrowhawk is a predator and hunts small birds in woodlands and over farmland. 4–6 eggs are laid in May on a nest of sticks built up a tree, usually next to the trunk.

▲ **Tawny owl** 38 cm
The tawny owl has soft wing feathers specially suited for silent flying at night. It hunts small mammals, birds and insects, especially beetles. 3–4 round, white eggs are laid in a hollow tree in April.

▲ **Willow warbler** 11 cm
Willow warblers are summer migrants arriving from Africa in April. They fly back in September. Most of their time is spent in the shrub layer where they search for insects. Up to 8 eggs are laid in May.

▲ **Green woodpecker** 32 cm
The green woodpecker has a loud laughing call as it flies from tree to tree. It eats insects on the bark and is also fond of ants which it captures on the ground with its long tongue. It digs a hole in a tree to lay its eggs.

▲ **Great spotted woodpecker** 23 cm
The great spotted woodpecker is a very handsome bird with a strong bill. It chips away the tree bark to get at insects and their larvae. 4–7 whitish eggs are laid in a hole in a tree during May.

▲ Coal tit 11 cm
The coal tit has a white patch on the back of its head. Common in coniferous woodland, it feeds largely on insects. The nest is usually built in a tree-hole where 6–10 eggs are laid during April–May.

▲ Long-eared owl 36 cm
The long-eared owl inhabits coniferous woodland. The tufts on its head are not its ears. It feeds at night on mice, voles, birds and insects. It lays 4–5 white eggs in an old nest of a pigeon or hawk.

▲ Siskin 11 cm
The siskin is found mostly in coniferous woodland. It is a bird of the tree tops and eats tree seeds and a few insects. The nest is built in a tree and 4–5 eggs are laid in April–June. The male (in front) is the more colourful.

▲ Nuthatch 14 cm
The nuthatch lives and feeds in the tree layer. It crawls along branches in search of insects but it will also eat seeds and berries. It wedges hazel nuts into the bark before chipping them open. Nuthatches nest in tree-holes.

▲ Tree creeper 13 cm
The tree creeper is also called the tree-mouse after the way it scuttles up tree trunks looking for insects. The nest is usually built behind a piece of loose, peeling bark. 5–9 eggs are laid in May or June.

▲ Pheasant Male 84 cm Female 59 cm
The pheasant is a game bird and was introduced from Asia about 200 years ago. They feed on shoots, seeds and insects. About 12 eggs are laid on the ground in April–June.

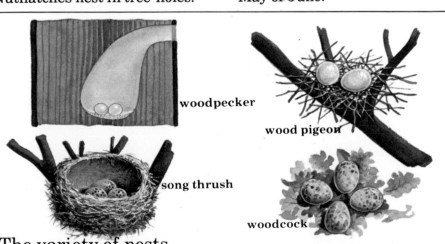

woodpecker

wood pigeon

song thrush

woodcock

The variety of nests

Woodpeckers dig out a hole in a tree trunk and lay their eggs on a bed of wood chips. Woodcocks' eggs are laid on the ground where they blend against a background of dead leaves.

Song thrushes build a cup-shaped nest of dead grasses and leaves and lined with mud. It is wedged in a forked branch. Wood pigeons construct a very flimsy platform of twigs in a tree or bush.

▲ Woodcock 34 cm
The woodcock is a native game bird. It nests and feeds on the ground. The long bill is pushed into soft soil or mud to capture worms. When disturbed it flies away very quickly and low, dodging between the trees.

Autumn

In autumn changes take place in the forest which help the plants and animals through the winter.

The breeding season is over. Migrant birds feed on the last swarms of insects. They must store enough energy for their long flights south. Caterpillars now pupate, forming a hard brown case over their soft skin. Some hang from little stalks in a crack in the tree bark but most simply drop to the ground. They will soon be covered with leaves which will keep them warm during the winter.

Many animals and birds use the huge crop of seeds, berries, fruit and nuts that are produced in autumn. The ground under oak trees becomes littered with acorns. Pigeons eat more acorns than any other bird.

In northern coniferous woods red squirrels and capercaillies feast on blue bilberries. Bright red hawthorn berries attract finches. Squirrels and jays bury nuts and acorns and return to them on mild winter days. Dormice store food in their cosy nests where they hibernate. The plants on the forest floor die back; mice and voles clamber through them looking for seeds.

Mammals put on weight and grow a thicker coat of fur. Autumn is their last chance to fill up with food before it becomes scarce. Red deer mate in the autumn.

During autumn the leaves of deciduous trees change colour, fall and pile up on the forest floor. Fungi push their way through the leaf litter. Some flies lay their eggs on toadstools and the larvae chew tunnels into the soft flesh. You may also see teeth marks on them from mammals.

The forest no longer hums with insect wings; most flying insects have laid their eggs and died. The rest shelter in their winter homes.

▲ Woodlands in autumn are very colourful. The leaves turn many different shades of red, orange and yellow before they fall.

▲ Bats hibernate hanging upside down, huddled together for warmth. They use hollow trees, caves or buildings to sleep in.

▲ Some toadstools grow in circles which are called fairy rings. As the fungus spreads underground so the ring widens each year.

▲ Squirrels and mice gnaw through the hard shell of hazel nuts. A small hole shows that a nut weevil has been inside.

Winter

The forest in winter is bleak. Trees stand bare; birds are quiet and many animals are asleep.

A thick blanket of dead leaves protects the soil from frost. Shrews tunnel under them searching for food. Each day they must eat their own weight in worms. Mice and voles rustle in the undergrowth nibbling at seeds.

Squirrels stay asleep when the weather turns cold but on mild days they set out to find the food they buried in autumn. Badgers may have already found some.

Winter is a bad time for birds. Flocks of tits, nuthatches and tree creepers inspect every twig, pecking quickly at dormant insects and their eggs. They are in a hurry. Winter days are short and there is less time to find what little food there is. At night they roost on a branch, feathers fluffed out to keep them warm.

Blackbirds and thrushes feed on the ground. They scratch through the leaves, turning them over and looking for insects underneath.

Footprints in the snow outside an earth show that a fox has been out to hunt for mice and voles. Scratches on a tree trunk show where badgers have sharpened their claws.

Moles have to dig deeper in winter to find worms which burrow far down into the soil. When moles find plenty of worms they bite and stun then and store them in underground larders.

There are no flowers to attract bees. Honey bees huddle in their nests to keep warm. They feed on honey stored during the summer. All the male bumble bees have died: only the queen lives through the winter. She is full of eggs and lays them in spring.

Many woodland plants have spent the winter as a bulb. As spring approaches they burst open to send out shoots.

▲ Male hazel catkins are called lambs' tails. They shake pollen into the wind which carries it to the red female flowers.

▲ Flocks of long-tailed tits search the tree tops for dormant insects and their eggs. Their feathers are fluffed to keep them warm.

▲ Bramblings visit the woods in Britain from their breeding grounds in northern Europe. Their favourite winter food is beech-mast.

▲ Frost and wind have stripped all the leaves from the trees. Now is a good time to look for animal tracks in the woods.

Looking up in coniferous woodland

Coniferous woodlands are darker, and usually quieter, than broad-leaved woodlands. Conifers grow very close to each other, whether in a natural forest or a plantation. There is therefore little light under the tree layer to allow many shrubs or ground plants to grow.

Rhododendron (8) bushes grow well in deep shade and they are often planted under conifers to give cover for game birds such as pheasants. Their pink flowers attract bees which collect the pollen and drink the nectar.

Two red deer stags (11) are fighting over females which are called hinds. They butt each other with their antlers in a trial of strength. Eventually the weaker stag tires and is chased away.

The goshawk (12) is a dashing hunter. It flies very quickly, dodging between the trees, to surprise and catch birds. Back at the nest it tears its prey into pieces, small enough for the chicks to swallow.

A goldcrest (19) is also feeding its young. The delicate cup-shaped nest is slung under a conifer branch and is built with moss, spiders' webs and feathers.

Coal tits (17) often lay their eggs in an old woodpecker's nest, but first they line the hole with feathers. They are very brave birds and sit tight on the eggs and hiss angrily should an enemy, such as a pine marten, try to rob the nest.

◄ A **squirrel** has used its sharp teeth to gnaw away the outside of this **pine cone**. It turns the cone in its fore-paws and nibbles the seeds in just the same way as we eat corn on the cob.

► **Pine sawfly larvae** feed on pine needles. They look like caterpillars but the adults are closely related to wasps.

A pine marten (**10**) is stalking a red squirrel (**9**). For the squirrel there is no escape in the trees because the pine marten is also a good climber and, like the squirrel, it has a bushy tail which helps it to balance. The pine marten also hunts birds in the trees and will eat their eggs and chicks.

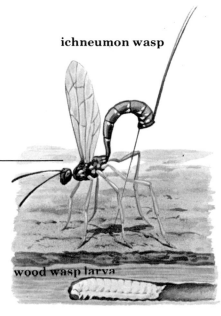

ichneumon wasp

wood wasp larva

▲ The **ichneumon wasp** uses its long egg-laying tube to bore a tiny hole into tree bark and deposite an egg on a larval wood wasp. When the egg hatches the ichneumon larva feeds on the wood wasp larva.

▼ The **crossbill** uses its curious twisted beak for opening pine cones to get at the seeds inside.

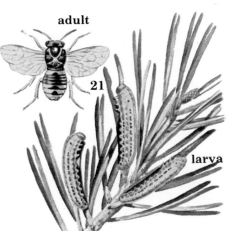

adult

larva

Key		11	Red deer
		12	Goshawk
1	Silver fir	13	Eagle owl
2	Larch	14	Great spotted
3	Spruce		woodpecker
4	Scots pine	15	Crossbill (male)
5	Birch	16	Crossbill (female)
6	Aspen	17	Coal tit
7	Rowan	18	Siskin
8	Rhododendron	19	Goldcrest
9	Red squirrel	20	Ichneumon wasp
10	Pine marten	21	Pine web sawfly

Trees of coniferous woodland

Coniferous woodland is dominated by evergreen trees which keep their leaves throughout the year. Many are important timber trees and are grown in plantations. The size and shape of the cone and the arrangement of the leaves are useful clues for their identification.

*Not to scale.

▲ Rowan or **Mountain ash**
Deciduous
Rowan has smooth, grey bark and seldom grows higher than 15 metres. Clusters of creamy white flowers open in May. By August the shiny red berries are ripe.

▲ Rhododendron Evergreen
A shrub which forms dense thickets, it is often planted to shelter breeding game birds. It grows best on poor, sandy soils. The pink or purple flowers, with brown spots, open in May-June.

▲ Silver fir Evergreen
Grows naturally in mountain ranges in central Europe but has also been widely planted. It grows up to 70 metres high. The needles are 1–2.5 cm long, thin and flat with two white stripes underneath.

▲ Aspen Deciduous
This tough tree can survive in cold mountain regions. The leaves flutter and tremble in the wind, showing grey underneath. Male and female catkins are borne on separate trees. The woolly seeds float away in June.

▲ Scots pine Evergreen
Huge forests of Scots Pine grow in northern Europe. The blue-green needles are 3–7 cm long and grow in pairs. Male cones shed pollen in May. The female cones take two years to ripen. The branches are rusty-red.

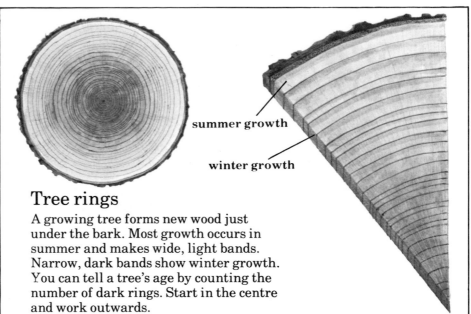

Tree rings

A growing tree forms new wood just under the bark. Most growth occurs in summer and makes wide, light bands. Narrow, dark bands show winter growth. You can tell a tree's age by counting the number of dark rings. Start in the centre and work outwards.

summer growth

winter growth

▲ **Douglas fir** Evergreen
This timber tree was brought over from America 150 years ago. It grows very quickly – to 30 metres in 30 years. The needles are 2–3 cm long. Douglas firs are known to live for over 750 years.

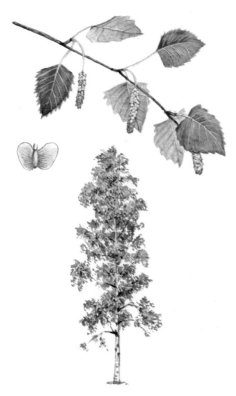

▲ **Silver birch** Deciduous
The trunk is covered with smooth, peeling white bark around dark, knobbly patches. The seeds have a delicate pair of wings and are blown from the female catkins in October. Birch trees only live for about 80 years.

▲ **Larch** Deciduous
Larch is very common in plantations. Bright green needles (2–3 cm long) sprout in March. The pinkish, young female cones appear in April. A larch tree can grow as much as 10 cm a week in summer.

▲ **Norway spruce** Evergreen
This tall, graceful tree is widely planted in northern Europe for timber and Christmas trees. The pale brown female cones grow up to 18 cm long. It has shallow roots and is easily blown over in gale force winds.

On the ground in coniferous woodland

Coniferous woods are usually very shady and the soil is often poor. The plants found on the woodland floor can thrive under these conditions. Bilberry (3) and cowberry (4) can only grow on poor soils. Creeping ladies' tresses (8), lesser wintergreen (10) and buckler fern (14) grow well in deep shade. A great variety of mushrooms and toadstools appear during autumn even in the darkest woods.

Wood ants (21) cover their underground nests with a huge mound of dead pine needles. This helps to keep the colony warm in winter during which they eat their stores of seeds. In summer they feed on insects, especially caterpillars. Worker ants travel high into the trees to collect them. If the nest is threatened they squirt stinging acid from tail glands at their attackers.

A black woodpecker (19) feeds on wood ants. It also hacks open rotting logs in search of insects. A capercaillie (18) struts through his territory uttering a loud rattling call that warns off rival males. The female lays 5–8 eggs at the base of a pine tree. Capercaillies eat the buds and shoots of young conifers as well as berries and seeds.

mite

springtails

◀ More than 200,000 **springtails** and **mites** can be found in one square metre of coniferous forest floor. They feed on the dead needles.

▶ The **puffball fungus** ripens into a dry bag which contains millions of tiny spores. Clouds of spores escape through an opening at the top and are carried away by the wind.

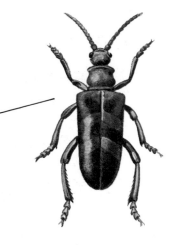

▲ The **two-banded longhorn beetle** (13-22 cm) is common in pine woods. Its larvae live and feed in rotting wood for 2 or 3 years before emerging as adults.

▼ The seeds of **cow-wheat** (**12**) are mistaken by **ants** for their pupae because they look so similar. Ants help to spread the seeds by carrying them back to their nest.

spores

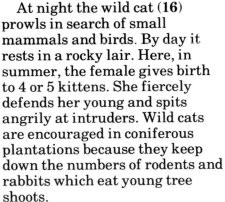

At night the wild cat (**16**) prowls in search of small mammals and birds. By day it rests in a rocky lair. Here, in summer, the female gives birth to 4 or 5 kittens. She fiercely defends her young and spits angrily at intruders. Wild cats are encouraged in coniferous plantations because they keep down the numbers of rodents and rabbits which eat young tree shoots.

Key

1	Bracken	22	Boletus
2	Bramble	23	Fly agaric
3	Bilberry	24	Puffball
4	Cowberry	25	Wood mushroom
5	Foxglove	26	False chanterelle
6	Heather		
7	Moss (*Hycolomium splendeus*)		
8	Creeping ladies' tresses		
9	Ball moss		
10	Lesser wintergreen		
11	Wavy hair grass		
12	Cow-wheat		
13	Polypody fern		
14	Buckler fern		
15	Polecat		
16	Wild cat		
17	Bank vole		
18	Capercaillie		
19	Black woodpecker		
20	Scotch argus butterfly		
21	Wood ants		

Insects and other tiny animals

Animals without backbones are called invertebrates. They cannot grow as big as birds or mammals because they have no skeleton to support them. There are thousands of different species of invertebrates in our woodlands. They feed on a great variety of foods and are themselves eaten by other animals.

*Not to scale. Average adult body length given. Ws = wingspan.

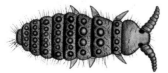

▲ **Springtail** 2mm
The springtail can jump by flicking the fork-shaped tail which is curled under its body. They are abundant in the soil and feed on dead leaves. They die in autumn and their eggs lie dormant through the winter.

▲ **Speckled wood butterfly** 14mm Wingspan 36mm
The speckled wood is very common. It can often be seen fluttering along woodland paths and in sunny clearings. It breeds throughout the summer. The green caterpillars eat grasses.

▲ **Wood white butterfly** 15mm Ws 35mm
The wood white is found on sunny days flying around paths and clearings. On dull days it clings to the underside of a leaf. The caterpillars eat plants of the pea family, such as vetch.

▲ **Purple hairstreak butterfly** 14mm Ws 35mm
The purple hairstreak flies high among the tree tops in July and August. It likes to feed on sweet chestnut flowers. The eggs are laid on oak leaves which the caterpillars eat.

▲ **Silver-washed fritillary butterfly** 22mm Ws 60mm
The silver-washed fritillary is found in woods where there are plenty of violets for its caterpillars to eat. The eggs are usually laid on an oak trunk.

▲ **Oak eggar moth** 20mm Ws 50mm
The oak eggar is a brown furry-bodied moth which flies in July and early August. The males fly by day as well as by night when the females are active. The caterpillars feed on bramble and hawthorn leaves.

▲ **Oak tortrix moth** 7mm Ws 18mm
The oak tortrix is a small nocturnal moth which is very common in oak woods. It flies in June and July. The eggs hatch in May and the caterpillars feed on oak leaves. It is also called the Green oak beauty.

▲ **Magpie moth** 18mm Ws 43mm
The magpie moth is very common and easy to recognize. It flies in July and August. The caterpillars feed on hawthorn, raspberry and gooseberry bushes and they are often found in gardens as well as woods.

► The eggs hatch in July.

1

The life cycle of the Purple Emperor

The caterpillars start feeding on leaves.

2

They hibernate in autumn in a silk cocoon. In spring they begin feeding and growing.

► In June they pupate – a hard case forms round them as they hang upside down from a stalk.

3

4

▲ After 2 weeks the case cracks open and the adult butterfly crawls out.

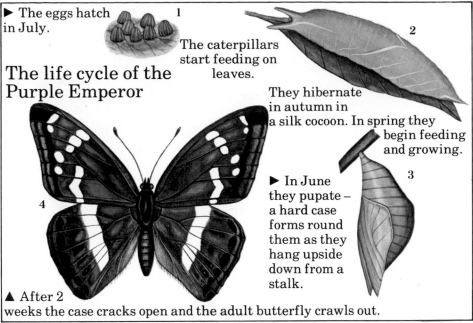
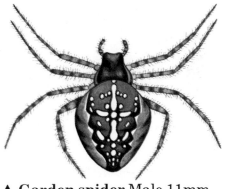

▲ **Garden spider** Male 11mm Female 20mm
The garden spider builds a web to catch flying insects. It has poison fangs and bites its victim to death. In autumn the female dies after laying eggs which hatch next spring.

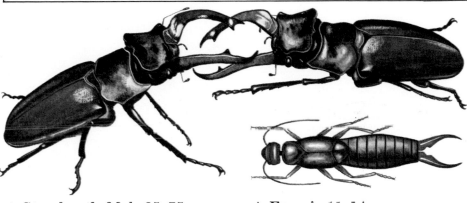
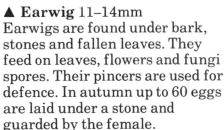

▲ **Stag beetle** Male 25–75mm Female 22–45mm
Stag beetles feed on sap oozing from wounds in oak bark. The males have upper jaws like antlers, and fight over females in summer. The eggs are laid on rotting wood where the larvae live.

▲ **Earwig** 11–14mm
Earwigs are found under bark, stones and fallen leaves. They feed on leaves, flowers and fungi spores. Their pincers are used for defence. In autumn up to 60 eggs are laid under a stone and guarded by the female.

▲ **Hedge snail** Shell width 17mm
Hedge snails are very common in and around woodlands where they feed on ground-level plant leaves. The shell colour can vary a great deal. In winter they hibernate in a hole in the soil.

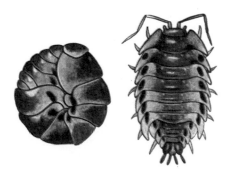

▲ **Millipede** 15–50mm
Millipedes live under logs and stones and they feed on dead plant remains. When alarmed they coil up as though they were dead. They can also squirt a stinking yellow liquid at their enemies.

▲ **Centipede** 20–30mm
The centipede is found amongst dead leaves and under logs and stones. It is a predator and feeds on spiders, woodlice and worms. It catches food with its front pair of legs which are poisonous pincers.

▲ **Woodlouse** 15mm
Woodlice live in the damper parts of woods and feed on dead plant remains. They hide under stones and behind bark and roll into a tight ball if disturbed. Woodlice are closely related to crabs and shrimps.

Plants without flowers

Woodlands contain a great variety of plants that never produce flowers or seed. They grow from tiny spores which are much smaller than the seeds of flowering plants. Large number of mushrooms and toadstools appear in autumn. Fungi like these digest dead leaves and rotting wood.

Do not eat or taste any wild fruit or fungi unless you are quite sure they are harmless. Fungi marked ! are very poisonous: do not touch.

▲ **Mosses** grow from spores released from tiny capsules which dry open in the wind and shake out their contents.

▲ Many lichens can be found on tree trunks or rocks but the **pixie cup** grows on the soil. Spores are formed around the rim of the cup.

▼ The *Pellia* liverwort grows on damp soil and wet rocks. The spore capsule grows from a curly green leaf called a thallus.

6

▲ The **male fern** sprouts from a large woody root. Under the fronds are clusters of spores.

▲ Flies eat the smelly slime of the **stinkhorn fungus** and spread its spores in their droppings.

▲ 'Umbrella' fungi have **gills**. Millions of minute spores fall from gaps between the gills.

▲ **Bird's nest fungi** spores form eggs which lie in the cup until raindrops wash them out.

16

Key		
1 Moss (*Dicranoweisia cirrata*)	7 Moss (*Brachythecium rutabulum*)	16 Hart's tongue fern
	8 Orange lichen	17 Sulphur tuft fungus
2 Liverwort (*Frullania dilatata*)	9 Lichen (*Parmelia caperata*)	18 Stinkhorn
		19 Bird's nest fungus
3 Moss (*Hypnum cupressiforme*)	10 Lungwort	20 Chanterelle
	11 Lichen (*Ramalina farinacea*)	21 Death cap (POISON)
4 Pixie cup lichen		22 Fly agaric (POISON)
5 Moss (*Dicranum scoparium*)	12 Male fern	23 Boletus
	13 Buckler fern	24 Sickener (POISON)
6 Liverwort (*Pellia epiphylla*)	14 Polypody fern	25 Wood blewit
	15 Hard fern	26 Saffron milk cap
		27 Bracket fungus (*Trametes versicolor*)

23

! 21

! 22

! 24

25

26

The web of life

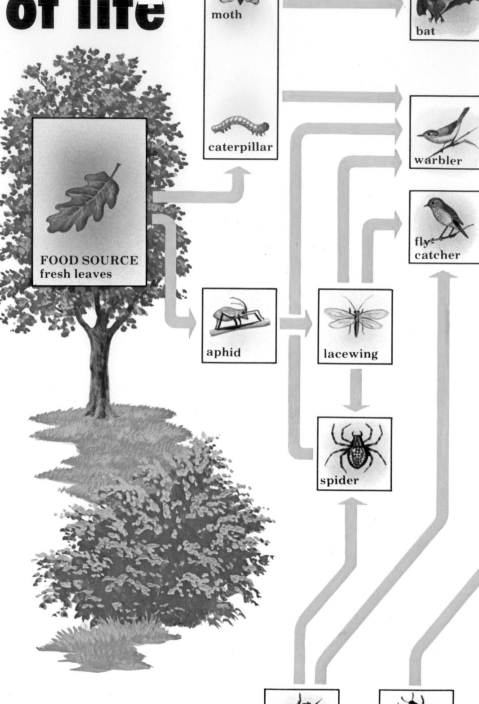

Food sources

All the living things in a wood depend on others for their food. Each, in turn, is food for other species.

The primary source of food is in plants. In a wood there are plant foods in the form of leaves, wood and fruits. Another source of food is the dead and decomposing remains of plants and animals.

Leaves

Leaves provide a great deal of the food – one oak tree may have over 100,000 leaves – so there are vast numbers of leaf-eating animals. Aphids, for example, suck leaf juices, and breed quickly in the summer when leaves are plentiful. Over 5,000 million aphids can live in one hectare of woodland. They can grow wings and fly away to search for new supplies if the leaves become too crowded. Aphids are eaten by lacewings, which in turn are eaten by spiders.

Caterpillars are tremendous leaf-eaters and are eaten by many birds. Migrants, such as warblers, fly all the way from Africa to raise their young in summer on the abundant supply of juicy caterpillars.

Other sources

Wood is a food for beetle larvae, which chew tunnels behind the bark. Even here they are not safe from woodpeckers.

Dead leaves and animals are an important source of food for 'decomposers'. Worms, for example, eat dead leaves and help make the soil fertile. In turn they provide food for birds and mammals.

The large quantities of seeds and fruits produced each year provide a feast for voles, wood mice, and birds such as chaffinches.

Food chains

As we have seen, warblers eat spiders which eat lacewings which eat aphids which feed on leaf juice. This list can be made into a food chain:

leaves-aphid-lacewing-spider-bird

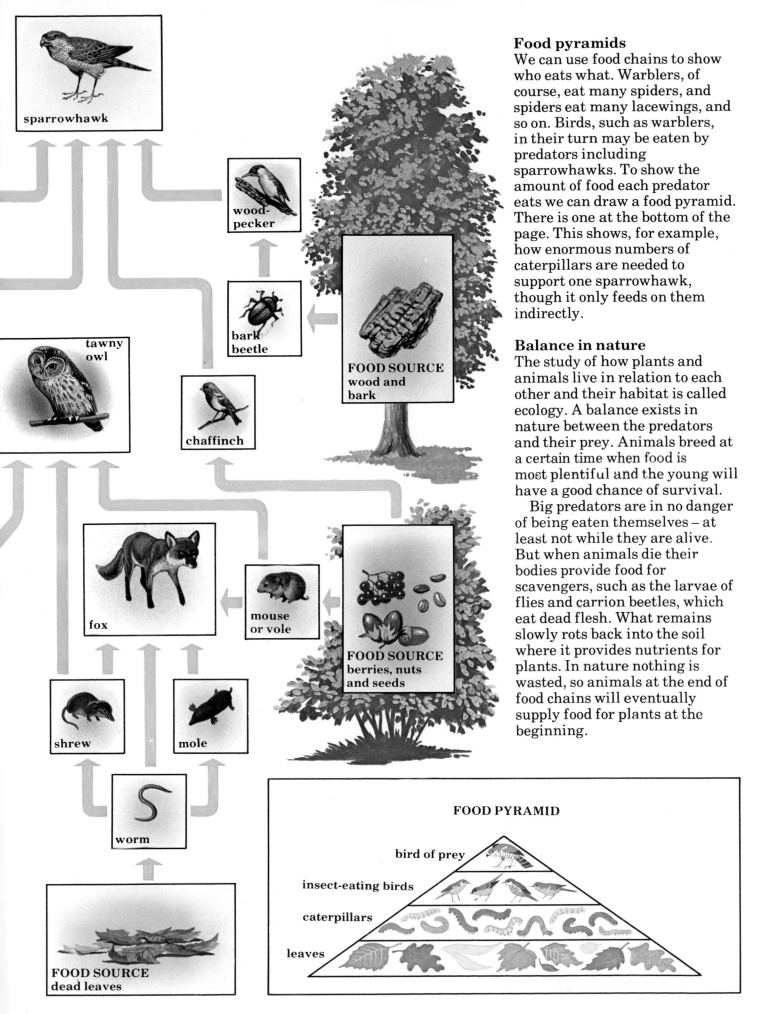

sparrowhawk

wood-pecker

bark beetle

FOOD SOURCE
wood and bark

tawny owl

chaffinch

fox

mouse or vole

FOOD SOURCE
berries, nuts and seeds

shrew

mole

worm

FOOD SOURCE
dead leaves

Food pyramids

We can use food chains to show who eats what. Warblers, of course, eat many spiders, and spiders eat many lacewings, and so on. Birds, such as warblers, in their turn may be eaten by predators including sparrowhawks. To show the amount of food each predator eats we can draw a food pyramid. There is one at the bottom of the page. This shows, for example, how enormous numbers of caterpillars are needed to support one sparrowhawk, though it only feeds on them indirectly.

Balance in nature

The study of how plants and animals live in relation to each other and their habitat is called ecology. A balance exists in nature between the predators and their prey. Animals breed at a certain time when food is most plentiful and the young will have a good chance of survival.

Big predators are in no danger of being eaten themselves – at least not while they are alive. But when animals die their bodies provide food for scavengers, such as the larvae of flies and carrion beetles, which eat dead flesh. What remains slowly rots back into the soil where it provides nutrients for plants. In nature nothing is wasted, so animals at the end of food chains will eventually supply food for plants at the beginning.

FOOD PYRAMID

bird of prey

insect-eating birds

caterpillars

leaves

Visiting woodlands

Planning your visit

You can have great fun exploring woods. Walking in woods is a pleasant and relaxing way of enjoying spectacular natural scenery; on your walk you can also learn much about the woodland ecosystem.

It pays to take a good map of the area so that you can find your way along the various paths. Most woodlands and plantations have public footpaths or tracks passing through, but you must ask the owner's permission to visit private woods.

How to approach a wood

Always remember that mammals and birds are shy and will be scared away if you make a noisy approach. Walk slowly, tread carefully and try not to snap twigs under foot. Wear stout boots and clothes in browns and greens which will match the surroundings. Take a waterproof anorak in case in rains.

Dogs love going for walks but they will frighten away animals if they go crashing through the undergrowth. Keep your dog under strict control if you want to see animals in the wild.

Wherever your path is crossed by another, approach the junction cautiously. If you are lucky, there may be deer feeding on the path to your left or right. If you spot deer, or any other animal, stay perfectly still.

Watching and listening

Binoculars are essential for watching birds and useful when studying mammals such as squirrels, rabbits and deer, that may be seen during the day. A very good idea is to sit beside a tree for about half an hour.

Animals are more likely to show themselves if you remain quiet and still. After a while you will be able to recognize different bird songs and calls and be able to tell which birds are around even if you cannot actually see them.

Do not disturb birds' nests. You will only frighten the parents who may then desert their eggs or chicks. It can also be dangerous – owls will sometimes attack people who threaten their nests. Never go rushing after birds as they will fly out of sight before you have had a proper look.

If you find a young bird out of its nest, do leave it where it is, and leave it alone. It will be waiting for its parents to return with food. If you move it, they may lose it or abandon it.

Winter and summer

In winter it is exciting to track animals along snow-covered woodland paths. You will be amazed at how many mammals and birds have crossed or walked along the same path as you. Look for places where the snow has been scraped away by animals searching for food.

Look for caterpillars on the leaves of bushes in summer. It is fun to keep a few at home in a large glass jar or old aquarium. You must provide them with plenty of food – leaves from the same kind of plant you found them on. Study their life cycles as they eat and grow, change into pupae, and finally emerge as adult moths or butterflies. Release them at this stage or they will soon die.

Look under rotting logs for beetles, woodlice and many other small animals.

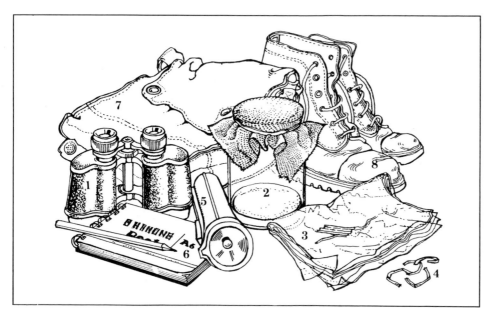

▲ **Useful things to take. Binoculars (1) for watching mammals and birds. One or two plastic or glass jars (2) for collecting caterpillars and other small animals. Plastic bags (3) and ties (4) for plant material. A torch (5) for night visits. A writing pad and pencil (6) for notes and drawings. A simple rucksack (7) is useful to carry your gear, and do wear stout boots (8) if you can.**

Watching badgers

In summer you can watch badgers come out from their setts at dusk. A farmer or gamekeeper will often tell you where to find them. Look for fresh footprints in the earth outside the entrances to make sure they are occupied. A good plan is to lay a row of twigs across each entrance, and return next day to see which holes the animals emerged from during the night – the twigs will be knocked down. These are the holes to watch. Be there at least an hour before sunset and sit somewhere with a good view. You may also see foxes, and bats hunting moths against the evening sky. Never go alone. It is best to go badger-watching with an adult but if you go with a friend tell an adult exactly where you are going and when you will return. Wear a watch so you do.

▼ **Badger-watching. Always note which way the wind is blowing. Badgers, like most animals, have a very keen sense of smell. They will be frightened away if the wind blows your scent towards them.**

Keeping a record

Try to learn the names of the plants you find. If you do not want to take a book with you, make a sketch with notes and look them up later. Don't uproot whole plants or pick large bunches of wild flowers.

If you make regular trips to woods you can build up your own woodland diary. Make notes about the plants, mammals, birds and insects you find through the seasons. Illustrate your nature notebook with sketch maps, drawings and paintings. Fungi, for instance, are quite easy to draw and fun to colour with crayons or paints. If you have a camera you might also include photographs of the woods you visit.

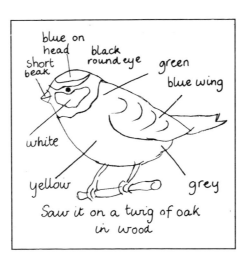

blue on head
short beak
black round eye
green
blue wing
white
yellow
grey

Saw it on a twig of oak in wood

▲ **If you spot a bird that you do not recognize, make a rough sketch with notes. Jot down the colour of its breast, head and wings. This will help you to identify it when reference books are handy.**

The Country code

Follow the country code and you will not give anyone cause to regret your woodland visits.

Guard against fire
Leave no litter – take your rubbish home
Keep dogs under proper control
Fasten all gates
Keep to paths across farmland
Avoid damaging fences, hedges and walls
Safeguard water supplies – don't pollute or throw rubbish into any pond, stream, river or ditch
Go carefully on country roads
Respect the life of the countryside
Protect wildlife, wild plants and trees

Word list

Antenna One of a pair of feelers on an insect's head which are its organs of smell and touch.

Canopy The 'ceiling' of a woodland formed by the layers of tree branches.

Carnivore An animal or plant that eats animals.

Deciduous A tree which loses its leaves in winter.

Diurnal Active by day.

Dominant species The most common animals or plants in a particular habitat.

Dormant Resting. Many plants and insects pass the winter in a dormant state.

Ecology The study of how plants and animals live together in their natural surroundings.

Ecosystem A distinct type of animal and plant community. Woodlands, grasslands, moorlands and freshwater habitats are separate ecosystems.

Evergreen A tree which does not lose its leaves in winter.

Foliage The leaves of plants.

Habitat The natural surroundings of a plant or animal.

Herbivore An animal that eats plants.

Hibernation Passing the winter in a deep sleep. Animals which hibernate store fat in their bodies to keep them alive.

Invertebrate An animal without a backbone. Insects, spiders, worms and snails are all invertebrates.

Larva The young stage of many animals. In insects, this is the feeding and growing stage between leaving the egg and becoming an adult.

Migration The movement of animals, usually with the change of season. Many birds migrate south in the winter.

Nocturnal Active at night.

Plumage The feather coat of birds.

Pollination The transfer of pollen from the male sex organs of flowers to the female sex organs so that fertilization is achieved.

Predator An animal that hunts and kills other animals for food.

Prey Animals that are eaten by predators.

Pupa Stage in insect development between larva and adult. The pupa, which usually has a hard covering, does not feed and is almost motionless.

Territory An area in which an animal breeds and gathers most of its food. Many birds fiercely defend their territories against intruders of the same species.

Vertebrate An animal with a backbone. Mammals and birds are vertebrates.

How to find out more

Clubs and societies

You can learn a great deal about nature by talking to people with similar interests; the best way of meeting them is to join a club or society. Many organize field trips and have regular meetings. Several have junior sections.

Always enclose a stamped, self-addressed envelope when writing for information.

County Naturalist Trusts are very active in wildlife conservation. They look after a great number of nature reserves which protect rare animals and plants. Members can often become involved in conservation work and other projects. You can obtain the address of your local Naturalist Trust from:
The Council for Nature
The Zoological Society
Regent's Park
London NW1 4RY.

The Royal Society for the Protection of Birds (RSPB) has a junior branch, the **Young Ornithologists Club** (YOC) which you can join if you are under 15. It arranges outings and meetings and produces a magazine called *Bird Life*. This contains articles by experts and members, information on competitions and projects, and club news. Members also receive a membership card and badge. The RSPB owns a number of nature reserves where some of our rarest birds can be seen. For more information write to:
RSPB
The Lodge
Sandy
Bedfordshire.

Watch is the environmental club for young people run by the *Sunday Times* and the **County Nature Conservation Trust**. Members receive the magazine *Watchword* 3 times a year. For more information write to:
Watch
22, The Green
Nettleham
Lincoln
LN2 2NR.

The Wildlife Youth Service is a branch of the **World Wildlife Fund**. Members are kept up to date with the latest wildlife conservation news and can take part in projects and field camps. For further details write to:
The Secretary
Marston Court
Manor Road
Wallington
Surrey.

Protecting Woodlands

The Forestry Commission is responsible for over 200 large forests and plantations, many set in the beautiful scenery of our National Parks. Nearly all let the public in. They also run a number of large **forest parks** where visitors can park, camp and picnic, and follow **nature trails**. For more information on these, and their wide range of publications on forests and wildlife, write to:
The Forestry Commission
231, Corstorphine Road
Edinburgh
Scotland.

Nearly 120,000 hectares of Britain's most important wildlife habitats, including woodlands, are protected by the **National Nature Reserves** set up by the **Nature Conservancy Council**. For more information write to:
Nature Conservancy Council
19, Belgrave Square
London.

Books

There are plenty of books about European wildlife. The ones listed here are only a small selection. It is a good idea to visit your local library and bookshop to see what else is available.

General

Guide to Watching Wildlife David Stephen (Collins);
The Family Naturalist Michael Chinery (Macdonald & Jane).

General – Woodlands

Woodlands William Condry (Collins Countryside series);
Exploring Woods Peter Schofield (Look-in/ITV Books);
The Natural History of an English Forest N. E. Hickin (Arrow).

Identification

The Collins Handguide to . . . (Collins);
The Observer Book of . . . (Warne);
The Usborne Spotter's Guide to . . . (Usborne).

Trees
A Field Guide to the Trees of Britain and Northern Europe Alan Mitchell (Collins);
Trees and Bushes of Europe Oleg Polunin (Paladin).

Flowering plants
The Concise British Flora in Colour W. Keble Martin (Ebury Press/Michael Joseph);
The Wildflowers of Britain and Northern Europe R. Fitter, A. Fitter and M. Blamey (Collins);
Wild Flowers of the Woodlands E. A. Ellis (Jarrold).

Plants without flowers
The Oxford Book of Flowerless Plants F. H. Brightman and B. E. Nicholson (Oxford University Press).
Mushrooms and Toadstools Ronald Rayner (Hamlyn).

Mammals
A Field Guide to the Mammals of Britain and Europe F. H. Van de Brink (Collins);
Carnivores of Europe Robert Burton (Batsford).

Birds
Birdwatchers' Pocket Guide Peter Hayman (RSPB/Mitchell Beazley);
A Field Guide to the Birds of Britain and Europe R. T. Peterson, G. Mountfort and P. A. D. Hollom (Collins).

Invertebrates
A Field Guide to the Insects of Britain and Northern Europe Michael Chinery (Collins);
Woodland Life G. Mandahl-Barth (Blandford).

Index